Signs of Life

Clip art for church, school & home life

Kourtney Harper

McCrimmons
Great Wakering, Essex, United Kingdom

Please take time to read this Licence Agreement

LICENSE AGREEMENT

Book International copyright law protects these images.
& CD McCrimmon Publishing Co. Ltd. understand that you have purchased this product so that you can use these images and incorporate them into another work. However there are restrictions on the use of these images (see Commercial Reproduction). McCrimmon Publishing Co. Ltd. gives you permission to copy and/or modify these images for use in a parish, school, community, institution or home use only.

Commercial reproduction

You cannot reproduce or make copies of any portion of the image collection for commercial distribution or resale. You may not copy, modify or distribute these images for commercial use, whether for profit or without profit, without the prior permission of the publisher.

CD ### Single user License Agreement

McCrimmon Publishing Co. Ltd. grant you this license for a single computer. You may not copy or duplicate the digital image files or documentation in any form or by any means, including electronic transmission. You may transfer your rights stated under this agreement for the digital image files and the accompanying written materials on a permanent basis provided you retain no copies and the recipient agrees to the terms of this agreement.

World Wide Web and Internet use

These images may not be used on the Internet or incorporated into a Website without the prior permission of the publisher.

Limited Warranty

McCrimmon Publishing Co. Ltd. warrant that the digital image files will perform substantially in accordance with the written instructions for a period of 60 days from the date of receipt. Any implied warranties are limited to 60 days. In no event shall McCrimmon Publishing Co. Ltd. or its suppliers be liable for any damages whatsoever arising out of the use of this product.
Statutory rights are not affected.

First published in the United Kingdom in 2001 by
MCCRIMMON PUBLISHING CO. LTD.
Great Wakering, Essex, SS3 0EQ

email: mccrimmons@dial.pipex.com
website: www.mccrimmons.com

ISBN 0 85597 630 6

British Library Cataloguing in Publication Data.
A catalogue record for this book is available from the British Library.

Illustrations by Kourtney Harper
Cover design and text page layout by Nick Snode
CD compilation and programming by Nick Snode
Printed and bound by Black Bear Press, Cambridge

Contents

Using the CD

Online Help

The online help within Portfolio requires Microsoft Internet Explorer or a similar internet browsing application to be installed on your computer to work properly.

Microsoft Internet Explorer can be downloaded from:
www.microsoft.com/downloads/
Netscape Communicator or Navigator can be downloaded from:
www.home.netscape.com/download/

Browsing software Portfolio Browser 5.0.1

No installation is required. The image catalogues are accessed directly from within the Portfolio Browser application on the CD.

Opening the image catalogues

W
M Open the CD

Read the Browser Quick Start Guide PDF file
If your computer has problems opening this file, install Acrobat Reader which can be found in the ☐ Adobe folder.

W Open the ☐ Portfolio Win Browser folder.

Open the PortBrws.exe application.

W
M At the Open Catalog window:
and in the Look-in window select your CD drive.

Open the Signs of Life catalogue you wish to browse:
SL_General
SL_Scriptural

Searching for images

There are several ways to find images within the Portfolio Browser catalogues:

Scrolling
Scroll up and down using the up and down arrows on the slider bar – select the image you want.

QuickFind

Type a word in the QuickFind text box – press Return or Enter. If the word entered matches any of the words in the Keywords list/field, the images will be displayed.

Find
Click the Find button on the tool bar.
In the first pop-up menu select:
> Keywords, or > Description,
in the second pop-up menu select: > contains,
in the third window type a word to search for and press Return or Enter.

Keywords
Click the list view button.

Double click a keyword to display all records with that keyword.

Find All

After performing any of the previous methods for finding an image, you must go to the menu bar and select > Cataloge > Find All.

Viewing the images

There are three ways to view the images within Portfolio Browser:

Thumbnail View
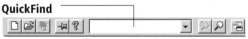
List View
Record View

Placing images into your document using Portfolio Browser

Open up your word processing or DTP document.

Open up a Portfolio Catalogue.
In Thumbnail View double click your selected image go to > Edit > Copy.

Go to your document and > Edit > Paste.

Placing images into your document without using Portfolio Browser

Choose an image from the book and make a note of the file name and category name.

W Example used: Microsoft Word *
In your word processing or DTP document go to > Insert > Picture > From File...

At the Insert Picture dialogue box and in the Look in window select your CD drive.

Open the Images folder.

Open the category folder and select the image you want.

* N.B. These instructions will be different depending on the application you are using.

File names explanation

Liturgical Year:

Year   Image no.   A01_AD1.TIF   Season   Sunday

Examples:

A05_CM1	–	Year A, 1st Sunday of Christmas
A20_ASH	–	Ash Wednesday
A21_LNT1	–	1st Sunday of Lent
A27_HT	–	Holy Thursday
A26_PASS	–	Passion/Palm Sunday
A28_GF	–	Good Friday
A29_EVIG	–	Easter Vigil
A30_ESUN	–	Easter Sunday
A31_EA2	–	2nd Sunday of Easter
A36_ASC	–	Ascension of the Lord
A38_PENT	–	Pentecost Sunday
A39_TRIN	–	Trinity Sunday
A40_OT09	–	9th Sunday in Ordinary Time
A65_XKNG	–	Christ the King

Activities

ACT001

ACT002

ACT003

ACT004

ACT005

ACT006

ACT007

ACT008

ACT009

ACT010

ACT011

ACT012

ACT013

ACT014

General

ACT015

ACT016

ACT017

ACT018

ACT019

ACT020

ACT021

ACT022

ACT023

ACT024

ACT025

ACT026

ACT027

ACT028

ACT029

General

ACT030

ACT031

ACT032

ACT033

ACT034

ACT035

ACT036

ACT037

ACT038

ACT039

ACT040

ACT041

ACT042

ACT043

ACT044

ACT045

ACT046   ACT047

Celebrations

CEL01

CEL02

CEL03

CEL04

CEL05

CEL06

CEL07

CEL08

CEL09

CEL10

CEL11

Charity

CHAR01

CHAR02

CHAR03

CHAR04

CHAR05

CHAR06

CHAR07

CHAR08

CHAR09

CHAR10

CHAR11

CHAR12

Church Business

BUS01

BUS02

BUS03

BUS04

BUS05

BUS06

BUS07

BUS08

BUS09

BUS10

BUS11

BUS12

BUS13

Family

FAM004

FAM005

FAM006

FAM007

FAM008

FAM009

FAM010

FAM011

FAM012

FAM013

FAM014

FAM015

FAM016

FAM017 · FAM018

FAM019 · FAM020 · FAM021 · FAM022

FAM023 · FAM024

FAM025

FAM026

FAM027

FAM028

FAM029

FAM030

FAM031 FAM032

FAM033

FAM034 FAM035

FAM036 FAM037

Holy Days & Holidays

HOL001

HOL002   HOL003   HOL004   HOL005

HOL006   HOL007

HOL008

HOL009

HOL010

HOL011

HOL012

HOL014

HOL013

HOL015

HOL016

HOL017

HOL018

HOL019

General

HOL100

HOL101

HOL102

HOL103

HOL104

HOL105

HOL106

HOL107

HOL108

HOL109

HOL110

HOL201

HOL202

HOL203

HOL207

General

HOL200

HOL204 HOL205 HOL206

HOL302

HOL300

HOL301

HOL208

HOL303

HOL304

Icons and Signs

IC001   IC002   IC003

IC004   IC005   IC006

Don't forget!

IC007   IC008   IC009

IC010

IC011

IC012

IC013

IC014

IC015

IC016

IC017

IC018

IC019

IC020

IC021

IC022

IC023

IC024

IC025

IC026

IC027

IC028

IC029

IC030

IC031

SIGN01

SIGN02

SIGN03

SIGN04   SIGN04W   SIGN05

SIGN06   SIGN06W

SIGN07   SIGN07W

SIGN08   SIGN08W

Ministries & Pilgrimages

MIN001

MIN002

MIN003

MIN004

MIN005

MIN006

MIN009

MIN008

MIN010

MIN012

MIN010A

MIN007

MIN011

MIN013

MIN014

MIN015

MIN016

MIN017

MIN018

MIN019

MIN020

MIN021

MIN022

MIN023

MIN024

MIN025

MIN026

MIN027

MIN028

MIN029

MIN031

MIN030

MIN033

MIN032

MIN034

MIN035

MIN037

MIN038

MIN036

PIL01

PIL02

PIL03

PIL04

Music

MUS01

MUS02

MUS03

MUS04

sing to the
Lord a new song

MUS05

MUS06

MUS07

MUS08

MUS09

MUS10

MUS11

MUS12

MUS13

MUS14

MUS15

MUS16

MUS17

MUS18

MUS19

MUS20

MUS21

MUS22

MUS23

MUS24

MUS25

MUS26

MUS27

Prayer

PRAY01

PRAY02

PRAY03

PRAY04

PRAY05

PRAY06

PRAY07

PRAY08

PRAY09

PRAY10

PRAY11

Sacraments

SAC001   Baptism / Christening

SAC002   Baptism / Christening

SAC003   Baptism / Christening

SAC004   Baptism / Christening

SAC005   Baptism / Christening

SAC006   Dedication

SAC007	Baptism	SAC008	Baptism

SAC009	Baptism	SAC010	Reconciliation

SAC011	Reconciliation	SAC012	Reconciliation

SAC013	Reconciliation	SAC014	Reconciliation

General

| SAC015 | Eucharist / Communion | SAC016 | Eucharist / Communion |

| SAC017 | Eucharist / Communion | SAC018 | Confirmation |

| SAC019 | Confirmation | SAC020 | Anointing the Sick |

| SAC021 | Anointing the Sick | SAC022 | Anointing the Sick |

| SAC023 | Anointing the Sick | SAC024 | Marriage |

| SAC025 | Marriage | SAC026 | Marriage |

| SAC027 | Marriage | SAC028 | Marriage |

SAC029 | Marriage

SAC031 | Ordination

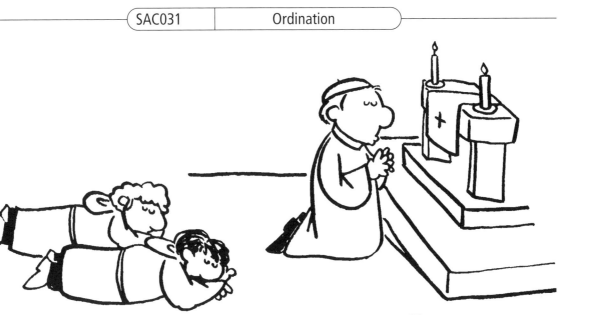

SAC030 | Ordination

Saints

ST001	Francis of Assisi	ST002	Paul the Apostle
ST003	Patrick	ST004	Virgin Mary
ST005	Joseph	ST006	John the Baptist

ST007	Matthew		ST008	Mark (symbol – winged lion)

ST009	Luke (symbol – winged ox)		ST010	John (symbol – eagle)

ST011	John (symbol – eagle)

School

SCH001   SCH002
SCH003   SCH004   SCH005
SCH006   SCH007

SCH008

SCH009

SCH010

SCH011

SCH012

SCH013

SCH014

Themes

TH007

TH008

TH009

TH010

TH011

TH012

TH013

Words

WRD01

God is Love.

God is Love.

WRD02

Seek ye first the kingdom of God...

WRD03

Prepare Ye... the Way of the Lord.

WRD04

For he is good, for his steadfast love endures forever.
-2 Chronicles 7.3

WRD05

You shall eat your fill and bless the Lord your God...
- Deuteronomy 8.10

WRD06

" I am who I am."
-Exodus 3.14

WRD13

Love one another.

WRD14

I am the Lord your God.

WRD07

The Lord our God we will serve, and him we will obey.
-Joshua 24.24

WRD09

Oh Happy Day!

WRD08

let your face shine on us...

WRD11

In the beginning was the Word:
the Word was with God and the Word was God.
He was with God in the beginning.
-John 1.1

WRD10

Whatever you eat,
whatever you drink,
whatever you do at all,
Do it for the glory of God.
. I Corinthians 10.31

WRD12

Follow me.
-John 21:19

WRD15

Know that I am with you always; yes to the end of time.

WRD16

Anyone who humbles himself will be exalted.
-Matthew 23

Liturgical Year – A

A01_AD1	1st Sunday of Advent

A02A_IMM	Immaculate Conception

A02B_IMM	Immaculate Conception

Let what you have said be done to me.

A02_AD2	2nd Sunday of Advent

A03_AD3	3rd Sunday of Advent

A04_AD4	4th Sunday of Advent

A05_CM1	Christmas

A07_CM3	Christmas

A08_HF	Holy Family

A06_CM2	Christmas

A09_MARY	Mary, Mother of God

A10_2CM	2nd Sunday after Christmas

No one has ever seen God;
it is the only Son, who is nearest
to the Father's heart,
who has made him known.
    -John 1

| A11_EPLD | Epiphany of the Lord | | A12_BAPL | Baptism of the Lord |

| A13_OT02 | 2nd Sunday in Ordinary Time |

There is the lamb of God that takes away the sin of the world. -John 1

| A14_OT03 | 3rd Sunday in Ordinary Time | | A15_OT04 | 4th Sunday in Ordinary Time |

| A16_OT05 | 5th Sunday in Ordinary Time | | A17_OT06 | 6th Sunday in Ordinary Time |

A18_OT07	7th Sunday in Ordinary Time

A19_OT08	8th Sunday in Ordinary Time

A20_ASH	Ash Wednesday

A21_LNT1	1st Sunday of Lent

A22_LNT2	2nd Sunday of Lent

A23_LNT3	3rd Sunday of Lent

A24_LNT4   4th Sunday of Lent   A25_LNT5   5th Sunday of Lent

A26_PASS   Passion Sunday   A28_GF   Good Friday

A29_EVIG   Easter Vigil

Scriptural

A27_HT   Holy Thursday

A30_ESUN	Easter Sunday

A31_EA2	2nd Sunday of Easter

He saw and he believed.
-John 20

A32_EA3	3rd Sunday of Easter

A33_EA4	4th Sunday of Easter

A34_EA5	5th Sunday of Easter

A36_ASC	Ascension

A37_EA7	7th Sunday of Easter

I have glorified you on earth
and finished the work that
you gave me to do.
-John 17

A35_EA6	6th Sunday of Easter

Anybody who loves me will
be loved by my Father.
-John 14

A38_PENT	Pentecost Sunday

A39_TRIN	Trinity Sunday

A40_OT09	9th Sunday in Ordinary Time

A41_OT10	10th Sunday in Ordinary Time

A42_OT11	11th Sunday in Ordinary Time

A43_OT12	12th Sunday in Ordinary Time

Proclaim that the kingdom of heaven is close at hand.
-Matthew 9.36

A45_OT14	14th Sunday in Ordinary Time

A44_OT13	13th Sunday in Ordinary Time

| A46_OT15 | 15th Sunday in Ordinary Time | | A47_OT16 | 16th Sunday in Ordinary Time |

| A48_OT17 | 17th Sunday in Ordinary Time | | A49_OT18 | 18th Sunday in Ordinary Time |

| A49_T18B | 18th Sunday in Ordinary Time | | A50_OT19 | 19th Sunday in Ordinary Time |

| A51_OT20 | 20th Sunday in Ordinary Time | | A52_OT21 | 21st Sunday in Ordinary Time |

| A53_OT22 | 22nd Sunday in Ordinary Time |

| A54_OT23 | 23rd Sunday in Ordinary Time |

Where two or three meet in my name,
I shall be there with them. -Matthew 18

| A55_OT24 | 24th Sunday in Ordinary Time |

| A56_OT25 | 25th Sunday in Ordinary Time |

Scriptural

| A57_OT26 | 26th Sunday in Ordinary Time |

| A58_OT27 | 27th Sunday in Ordinary Time |

| A59_OT28 | 28th Sunday in Ordinary Time |

| A60_OT29 | 29th Sunday in Ordinary Time |

| A61_OT30 | 30th Sunday in Ordinary Time |

LOVE YOUR NEIGHBOUR AS YOURSELF.
-Matthew 22

| A64_OT33 | 33rd Sunday in Ordinary Time |

| A62_OT31 | 31st Sunday in Ordinary Time |

| A65_XKNG | Christ the King |

| A63_OT32 | 32nd Sunday in Ordinary Time |

Liturgical Year – B

| B01_AD1 | 1st Sunday of Advent | | B02A_IMM | Immaculate Conception |

| B02B_IMM | Immaculate Conception | | B02_AD2 | 2nd Sunday of Advent |

| B03_AD3 | 3rd Sunday of Advent | | B04_AD4 | 4th Sunday of Advent |

B05_CM1	Christmas Midnight Mass

B06_CM2	Christmas Dawn Mass

for a larger image see A06_CM2, page 64

B07_CM3	Christmas Daytime Mass

B08_HF01	Holy Family

B09_MAR1	Mary, Mother of God

B10A_2CM	2nd Sunday after Christmas

B10B_2CM	2nd Sunday after Christmas

In the beginning was the Word:
the Word was with God and the Word was God.
He was with God in the beginning.
-John 1.1

B11_EPLD | Epiphany of the Lord

B12_BAPL | Baptism of the Lord

B13_OT2 | 2nd Sunday in Ordinary Time

B14_OT3A | 3rd Sunday in Ordinary Time

B14_OT3B | 3rd Sunday in Ordinary Time

B15_OT4 | 4th Sunday in Ordinary Time

B17_OT6A | 6th Sunday in Ordinary Time

B16_OT5 | 5th Sunday in Ordinary Time

B17_OT6B | 6th Sunday in Ordinary Time

B19_OT8 | 8th Sunday in Ordinary Time

B18_OT7 | 7th Sunday in Ordinary Time

B20_ASH | Ash Wednesday

Scriptural

| B21_LNT1 | 1st Sunday of Lent | | B22_LN2A | 2nd Sunday of Lent |

| B22_LN2B | 2nd Sunday of Lent |

| B23_LN3A | 3rd Sunday of Lent |

| B23_LN3B | 3rd Sunday of Lent |

| B24_LNT4 | 4th Sunday of Lent | B25_LNT5 | 5th Sunday of Lent |

The man who lives by the truth comes out into the light, so that it may be plainly seen that what he does is done in God.
-John 3

| B26_PASS | Passion Sunday | B27_HTB | Holy Thursday |

| B27_HTA | Holy Thursday |

| B28_GFRI | Good Friday | B29_EVIG | Easter Vigil |

| B30_ESUN | Easter Sunday | B31_EA2 | 2nd Sunday of Easter |

| B32_EA3 | 3rd Sunday of Easter | B33_EA4 | 4th Sunday of Easter |

| B34_EA5 | 5th Sunday of Easter | B35_EA6 | 6th Sunday of Easter |

| B36_ASC | Ascension | B37_EA7 | 7th Sunday of Easter |

| B38_PENT | Pentecost Sunday |

| B39_TRIN | Trinity Sunday |

| B40A_COR | Corpus Christi |

| B40B_PP | Peter and Paul |

| B40_OT9A | 9th Sunday in Ordinary Time |

| B40_OT9B | 9th Sunday in Ordinary Time |

| B40_OT9C | 9th Sunday in Ordinary Time |

| B41_OT10 | 10th Sunday in Ordinary Time |

Scriptural

B42_OT11 | 11th Sunday in Ordinary Time

B44_OT13 | 13th Sunday in Ordinary Time

B45_OT14 | 14th Sunday in Ordinary Time

B43_OT12 | 12th Sunday in Ordinary Time

B46_OT15	15th Sunday in Ordinary Time

B46_T15B	15th Sunday in Ordinary Time

B47_OT16	16th Sunday in Ordinary Time

B48_OT17	17th Sunday in Ordinary Time

B49_OT18	18th Sunday in Ordinary Time

B49_T18B	18th Sunday in Ordinary Time

I am the bread of life.
He who comes to me will never be hungry;
He who believes in me will never thirst.
-John 6

B50_OT19	19th Sunday in Ordinary Time

B51_OT20	20th Sunday in Ordinary Time

| B52_OT21 | 21st Sunday in Ordinary Time | B53_OT22 | 22nd Sunday in Ordinary Time |

| B54_OT23 | 23rd Sunday in Ordinary Time | B55_OT24 | 24th Sunday in Ordinary Time |

| B56_OT25 | 25th Sunday in Ordinary Time |

| B57_OT26 | 26th Sunday in Ordinary Time |

B58_OT27	27th Sunday in Ordinary Time

B59_OT28	28th Sunday in Ordinary Time

B60_OT29	29th Sunday in Ordinary Time

B60_T29B	29th Sunday in Ordinary Time

B61_OT30	30th Sunday in Ordinary Time

B61_T30B	30th Sunday in Ordinary Time

B62_OT31	31st Sunday in Ordinary Time

You must love your neighbour as yourself.
There is no commandment greater than this.
—Mark 12

| B63_OT32 | 32nd Sunday in Ordinary Time | B64_OT33 | 33rd Sunday in Ordinary Time |

| B65_XKNG | Christ the King |

Liturgical Year – C

C01_AD1	1st Sunday of Advent

C02A_IMM	Immaculate Conception

C02_AD2	2nd Sunday of Advent

Prepare a way for the Lord,
make his paths straight.
Every valley will be filled in,
every mountain and hill be laid low,
winding ways will be straightened
and rough roads made smooth.
-Luke 3

C03_AD3	3rd Sunday of Advent

C04_AD4	4th Sunday of Advent

C05_CM1	Christmas Midnight Mass

C06_CM2	Christmas Dawn Mass

C07_CM3	Christmas Daytime Mass

C08_HF	Holy Family

The Word was the true light that enlightens all men.

C09_MARY	Mary, Mother of God

| C10_2CM | 2nd Sunday after Christmas |

The Word was the true light that enlightens all men.

| C11_EPLD | Epiphany of the Lord |

| C12_BAPL | Baptism of the Lord |

| C13_OT02 | 2nd Sunday in Ordinary Time |

| C14_OT03 | 3rd Sunday in Ordinary Time |

| C15_OT04 | 4th Sunday in Ordinary Time |

| C16_OT05 | 5th Sunday in Ordinary Time |

Scriptural

C17_OT06	6th Sunday in Ordinary Time

C18_OT07	7th Sunday in Ordinary Time

How happy are you who are poor; Yours is the kingdom of God.

C19_OT08	8th Sunday in Ordinary Time

C20_ASH	Ash Wednesday

Now is the favourable time; this is the day of salvation.
2 Corinthians 5

C22_LNT2	2nd Sunday of Lent

C21_LNT1	1st Sunday of Lent

C23_LNT3	3rd Sunday of Lent

(C24_LNT4 | 4th Sunday of Lent) — (C25_LNT5 | 5th Sunday of Lent)

(C27_HT | Holy Thursday)

(C26_PASS | Passion Sunday)

| C28_GF | Good Friday | | C29_EVIG | Easter Vigil |

| C30_ESUN | Easter Sunday |

| C31_EA2 | 2nd Sunday of Easter | | C32_EA3 | 3rd Sunday of Easter |

| C33_EA4 | 4th Sunday of Easter | | C34_EA5 | 5th Sunday of Easter |

C35_EA6 — 6th Sunday of Easter — C36_ASC — Ascension

My word is not my own: it is the word of the one who sent me.   John 14

C37_EA7 — 7th Sunday of Easter

Scriptural

C38_PENT — Pentecost Sunday

C39_TRIN — Trinity Sunday

When the Spirit of truth comes he will lead you to the complete truth.
-John 16:12

| C40_CORX | Corpus Christi | | C40_OT09 | 9th Sunday in Ordinary Time |

| C41_OT10 | 10th Sunday in Ordinary Time | | C42_OT11 | 11th Sunday in Ordinary Time |

| C43_JBAP | John the Baptist | | C43_OT12 | 12th Sunday in Ordinary Time |

| C44_OT13 | 13th Sunday in Ordinary Time | | C45_OT14 | 14th Sunday in Ordinary Time |

Rejoice rather that your names are written in heaven.
-Luke 10

C46_OT15	15th Sunday in Ordinary Time

C47_OT16	16th Sunday in Ordinary Time

C48_OT17	17th Sunday in Ordinary Time

C49_OT18	18th Sunday in Ordinary Time

C50_OT19	19th Sunday in Ordinary Time

C51_OT20	20th Sunday in Ordinary Time

C52_OT21	21st Sunday in Ordinary Time

C53_OT22	22nd Sunday in Ordinary Time

C54_OT23	23rd Sunday in Ordinary Time

C55_OT24	24th Sunday in Ordinary Time

C56_OT25	25th Sunday in Ordinary Time

C57_OT26	26th Sunday in Ordinary Time

C58_OT27	27th Sunday in Ordinary Time

C59_OT28	28th Sunday in Ordinary Time

C60_OT29	29th Sunday in Ordinary Time

| C61A_T30 | 30th Sunday in Ordinary Time |

| C61B_ASS | All Saints |

Rejoice and be glad.

| C64_OT33 | 33rd Sunday in Ordinary Time |

| C62_OT31 | 31st Sunday in Ordinary Time |

| C65_XKNG | Christ the King |

Scriptural

| C61C_ASS | All Saints |

Happy the pure in heart: they shall see God.

| C63_OT32 | 32nd Sunday in Ordinary Time |

Old Testament

OT001	Eve and the serpent	OT002	Adam and Eve

OT004	Naming the animals	OT003	Adam / Naked

OT005	Cain and Abel	OT006	Noah and the Ark

OT007	Noah counting the animals

OT008	Noah and the flood

Scriptural

| OT009 | Building the Tower of Babylon | OT010 | Building the Tower of Babylon |

| OT011 | Tower of Babylon | OT012 | God's promise to Abraham |

OT013	God's promise to Abraham

OT014	Lot's wife looks back

OT015	Abraham, Sarah and Isaac

OT016	Abraham and Isaac

OT017	Rebekah

OT018	Isaac meets Rebekah

OT019 — Jacob deceives Abraham

OT020 — Joseph and his brothers

OT021 — Joseph is sold by his brothers

OT022 — Joseph and Pharaoh's dreams

OT023 — Joseph and his brothers

OT024 — Moses in the reeds

OT025 — Moses and the burning bush

OT026 — Moses and the burning bush

| OT027 | Aaron's staff / snake | | OT028 | Egypt / Firstborn |

| OT029 | Moses parts the Red Sea | | OT030 | Pharaoh drowns |

| OT031 | Moses leads the Israelites | | OT032 | Manna from heaven |

| OT033 | The Ten Commandments | | OT034 | Worshipping false gods |

OT035	Walls of Jerichco

OT036	Samson and the jawbone

OT037	Samson / Gates of Gaza

OT038	Samson is bound

OT039	Anointing of David

OT040	David and slingshot

OT041	David and Goliath

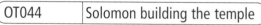

OT042	King David

OT043	David prays

OT044	Solomon building the temple

OT045	Elijah

OT046	Judith cuts head off Holofernes

OT047	Jeremiah

OT048	Jeremiah and potter's house

OT049	Jeremiah and the dry well

OT050	Shadrach, Meshach, Abednego

OT051	Daniel and the lion's den

OT052	Old Testament Shepherd

OT053	Psalm 104:16-17

OT054	Trumpeter		OT055	Oil lamps

OT056	Prophet / Teacher / Rabbi		OT057	Offering / Sacrifice

Scriptural

New Testament

NT_MARY1 | Mary / Immaculate Conception — NT_MARY2 | Mary and baby Jesus

NT_JOSEP | Joseph and Jesus — NT_JOHNB | John the Baptist is arrested

NT_JESUS | Jesus reads from the scrolls — NT_SCROL | Jesus reads from the scrolls

| NT_PROD1 | The Prodigal Son | | NT_PROD2 | The Prodigal Son |

| NT_SICK | Healing of the sick | | NT_COMF | Jesus comforts his people |

Scriptural

| NT_SOWER | The Sower | | NT_WATER | Jesus walks on the water |

NT_SHEP | The Good Shepherd

NT_TEMPL | Jesus in the temple

NT_VINE | I am the true vine

NT_HIPRT | High Priest

NT_PHAR | Pharisees plot against Jesus

Scriptural

| NT_ARRST | Arrest of Jesus | NT_CROW | Cock crows three times |

| NT_PETER | Peter denies Jesus | NT_PIETA | Mary's love for Jesus |

| NT_SPEAK | Jesus speaks | NT_STIGM | Jesus reveals his wounds |

Final events in the life of Jesus

including The Stations of the Cross

SX1 – indicates Station of the Cross

| SC01 | Judas betrays Jesus | | SC03 | Jesus predicts Peter's denial |

| | SC02 | The Last Supper | |

| SC04 | Jesus weeps | | SC05 | Desciples / Stay awake |

Scriptural

| SC06 | Jesus prays | | SC07 | Judas kisses Jesus / Betrayal |

| SC08 | Jesus arrested | | SC09 | Peter cuts the servant's ear |

| SC10 | Jesus is flogged | | SC11 | Pilate's indecision |

| SC12 | Jesus is condemned | | SC13 | Jesus taunted / crown of thorns |

SX1

SC14 | Jesus takes up his cross
SX2

SC14A | Jesus carrying his cross

SC15 | Jesus falls the first time
SX3

SC16 | Jesus meets his mother
SX4

SC17 | Simon of Cyrene carries the cross
SX5

SC18 | Veronica wipes the face of Jesus
SX6

SC19 | Jesus falls the second time
SX7

SC20 | Jesus meets the women of Jerusalem
SX8

Scriptural

| SC21 | Jesus falls the third time | SC22 | Jesus is stripped of his clothes |

SX9

SX10

| SC23 | Soldiers divide Jesus' clothes | SC24 | Jesus is nailed to the cross |

SX11

| SC25 | Jesus speaks to his mother | SC26 | Jesus is offered a drink |

SX12

| SC27 | Jesus cries out | SC28 | Jesus speaks to a thief |

My God, my God, why have you forsaken me?

SC29 — Jesus dies on the cross

SC30 — Jesus is removed from the cross

SC31 — Jesus is buried

SC32 — Jesus is risen / Resurrection